Full-Time Parent...Part-Time Coach!

*A Practical Guide for How to Be a Caring,
Fun, and Fair Youth Sports Coach*

FULL-TIME
PARENT...
PART-TIME
COACH!

A Practical Guide for
How to Be a Caring, Fun, and
Fair Youth Sports Coach

JOHN SHERTZER
JERRY TOOMER
BEN CECCHINI

Paperback ISBN 978-0-578-70645-0

1 3 5 7 9 10 8 6 4 2

Kudos!

I have witnessed every level of competitive athletics through my basketball journey. I cannot overstate how integral my parents were to my experience. My parents were as much an influence as any coach I had on the hardwood. As a parent myself, I hope to pass along the same lessons of enthusiasm, positivity, and effort to my own kids who have started their journey on sports. Catalytic coaches, like catalytic parents, are difference makers.

SHANE BATTIER
College and NBA Player
Executive and Head of Player
Development, Miami Heat

The guide fills a great need for *parents as coaches* to have the resources and practical ideas for teaching team skills. The guide provides real value in learning how to coach and provides practical ideas to strengthen your coaching skills. I personally have experienced coaching in youth leagues as well as at the National Team level with USA Basketball and know this guide will provide practical and immediately applicable ideas. I highly recommend all coaches, and parents, read this guide!

DON SHOWALTER
Director and Coach, USA Basketball

This book is a must-read for all parents "recruited" to coach their child's youth team. This book goes beyond fundamental skills and emphasizes the importance of social-emotional learning and character development necessary to build a positive learning environment. Youth coaches are often given only a team roster, schedule, and basic equipment when tasked with coaching their teams. Youth sports leagues, young athletes, and their families would benefit tremendously if this book were also provided to coaches at the onset of their seasons.

GRAHAM AND DR. SARAH HONAKER
University Development Officer
Pediatric Psychologist

I recall being asked to coach a team of 4-year olds for a YMCA soccer mini-camp. I knew nothing about soccer, and had enough trouble corralling my 4-year old let alone coaching 5 of them! The focus was solely on having fun, kicking the ball into the net and celebrating with snacks. As a parent, it was really important for me to understand my kids' coach's philosophy, so I wasn't confused as to why they make the choices they did, and to ensure they were making the experience enjoyable. A coach that can teach their team how to celebrate wins respectfully and power through losses with grace and determination has taught my child more than a specific sport skill—they have taught a life skill.

ANNETTE COULOMBE
Regional Marketing Director, Mom

This book captures unique and critical elements of the importance of social-emotional and character growth and provides evidence that coaching is much more than developing physical skills to win. Find the catalyst in you and your team through the journey of Becoming a Catalytic Coach!

NANCY MANDERFELD
Recipient of the Minnesota
National Girls and Women's
Sports Day Special Merit Award
Multi-sport Athlete and Coach

The authors remind us of the foundations of coaching and the long-lasting impact it can have on the young players. This book provides a practical guide to achieving real success, not just wins, through understanding, trust and teamwork.

This book serves as a guide as to how to incorporate the important developmental and cognitive aspect of coaching, guiding and motivating the youth of today. What kind of coach are you?

DENVER MCMAHON
Youth Coach
JILL MCMAHON
LCP, Child Therapist

This is a welcome guide for all of us who've been tapped to coach and may not feel completely prepared to step into the roles of teacher, motivator, encourager, and more. As a parent of athletes, a Division I collegiate athlete myself, and a youth coach (in a sport I hadn't mastered), I know how important coaches are and the challenges of leading young people. I wish I had had this book a long time ago.

BRENDA H. FREIJE
Consultant and Legal Advisor to
Nonprofits, Leadership Coach

I love the ideas and practical suggestions in this Guide. Whether you are a first time parent-coach, or a coach with a few years of experience, you will appreciate learning about effective and creative approaches to working with your young players. Examples range from a introductory season email from the coach ...to end of season feedback examples... to specific "soft skill" drills for a variety of team sports. I wish I would have had this book as a resource when I coached my kids!

DOUG REICHARDT
Chair of the Iowa Sports Foundation
for over 25 years, Athlete, Author

As parents, we 'coach' our kids each and every day. However, making the transition to a coach on the court, on the field, or in the gym can feel totally foreign to a lot of parents This highly practical book is a great resource for parents who take on the additional responsibilities of being a coach. Applying the catalytic framework gives parents and coaches an insightful roadmap on how to inspire and lead their children and teams.

LAVALL JORDAN
Head Coach
Butler University Men's Basketball

Table of Contents

Appreciation from the Authors

We would like to extend special thanks to the many coaches and parents who provided valuable ideas and examples for the book. Sharing their ideas and stories is a gift to us as authors and to you as readers. In particular, a shout out goes to: Eric Allen, Jay Baker, Shane Battier, Annette Coulombe, Cindy DeWitt, Lee Dicklitch, Pat Donahue, Bettye Ellison, Fritz Ettl, Brenda Freije, Lavall Jordan, Graham Honaker, Deb Lecklider, Nancy Manderfeld, Ryan McFarland, Mindy Ostrander, Maggie Pilloton, Doug Reichardt, Scott Rush Courtney Salati, Don Showalter, Ron Thomas, Chris Toomer, Scott Troyer, Vicki and Marty Wilke, and Andy Zidron.

Special thanks to our editing partner Jeanne Glasser Levine for helping make our ideas come to life.

Appreciation from the Authors

Preface

The idea for this book, perhaps more appropriately called a *guide*, was sparked by readers of *The Catalyst Effect:12 Skills and Behaviors to Boost Your Impact and Elevate Team Performance*, Toomer et al. (Emerald Publishing, 2018). The central theme in that book and the field research behind it is "leading from wherever you are." The core concept of leading without having an official title or position of authority formed the basis for the 12 key competencies that are described in detail in the book.

In our discussions with leaders in sports, arts, and business about the Catalyst Effect model, we were asked whether it made sense to teach the core competencies to youth in recreational settings as well as their coaches. Our answer was *yes*! Many of the examples of catalysts that we heard about in our interviews and workshop discussions related directly back to sports teams. With that in mind, our goal has been to gather expert input from experienced parents and coaches as to how to best teach these *soft skills* to younger players–and then to share them in a straightforward, practical guide for coaches.

The Call

Perhaps you have received *the call* from a league co-ordinator, "We need a parent to volunteer to coach your child's team." If you are a first-time coach, the challenge is especially daunting–the concern about not being effective or successful is high. Where can I go to find resources as to how to coach effectively? Where can I find both technical, physical skill based drills AND also specific ideas for teaching the *soft skills* to my players?

With that in mind, we hope that this guide provides ideas and tools pertaining to the soft skills that are useful to you as either a first-time coach or an experienced coach who is actively seeking to incorporate new ideas. For additional suggestions or to connect with us, you can reach us at thecatalysteffect.org or givengrowbasketball.org.

We thank you for taking time to read the book and for playing a key role in the development of young athletes:

- John Shertzer: Parent, Coach, Author, Executive Director, Society of Professional Journalists.

- Jerry Toomer: Parent, Coach, Author of *The Catalyst Effect* and Adjunct Professor at Butler University.

- Ben Cecchini: Athlete, Mental Skills Trainer, Coach, Partner at Give N' Grow Basketball.

CHAPTER 1

Yikes, I'm the Coach!

"Anyone who attempts is not a failure." – Sarah Dessen, Author

We were down 6-5 in the opening round of the playoffs. Somehow, we managed to get three outs in the top of the inning to keep it at a one-run deficit. The scorebooks flipped to the bottom of the 6th, final inning, and I heard my son excitedly chattering in the dugout about the fact that our four best hitters were due up (frankly, we only had four good reliable hitters). I was excited too, and my jog from the dugout to the 3rd-base coach position had more spring and bounce than usual.

I played it out in my mind: the scrappy Pirates, the worst team in the Zionsville Little League Majors Division were about to set field #2 ablaze with an upset over the Giants that would wipe away the disappointment of the previous 12 games. And in dramatic fashion no less.

I was worried, but also welcomed a fleeting feeling of relief. If we pulled this off, the struggles of my first-ever head coaching experience would fly away like the dust blowing off the field. I could push aside the doubts I had about my egalitarian approach to move the batting lineup around so much and let any kid who wanted to pitch take the mound. That had led to a record of 1-11. We couldn't buy a win. Near the end of the year I tried more conventional methods and yet we lost heartbreakers, and became the constant recipients of dramatic wins by our opponents. As the June Indiana heat began to ramp up, so did the losses, and my team of 5th- and 6th-graders grew demoralized.

But yet, that could all change right now. We had prepared for the playoffs, and here we were, 1 run from a tie game, and 2 runs from a walk-off win.

This was our moment.

Batter #1 swung at the first pitch and the ball went high up into the sky and landed peacefully in the centerfielder's glove.

Still our moment.

Batter #2 struck out on 3 pitches.

Still…

Batter #3 hit a weak ground ball to a very capable second baseman, who easily flipped it to first.

Our final record was 1-12.

This story by one of our authors illustrates the trials and tribulations of a youth sports coach. We've written this book for coaches new to the endeavor and who are trying extremely hard to create a positive experience for the kids. Have you been the victim of the "if you don't coach, we can't field a team" guilt trip, or the persistence of a child who thinks their mom or dad can be the next Pat Summitt, the next Brad Stevens? The author in this story was the latter—his son kept begging John to coach.

A humorous side note: John's dad coached one of his little league teams when he was a kid, and he only won one game that year as well. As John, recalls "I still remember the look on my dad's face when we won that game and I'll forever love him for it! Regardless of whether you win one game or ten during the season, this book is meant to help people like the Shertzers, for whom clipboards and whistles were strange devices."

Both experienced and inexperienced coaches will find this book valuable. Even if you have been the head coach for a dozen teams, but are committed to getting better, we will provide unique, useful ideas that will improve your effectiveness. This is especially true if you have a desire to elevate the social-emotional growth and character development of your players. For instance, you want one of your volleyball players to master their role in the 6-position–and *also* learn how to be a catalytic teammate. Or, you want your soccer players to deliver beautiful back-heel kicks–and *also* learn to be shining examples of teammates who build camaraderie. If so, you will enjoy this book. You will learn practical approaches and tools that will increase your effectiveness and very likely your personal satisfaction in serving young players and families.

The Parents

Let's not forget the parents! While coaching youth sports is a challenge, it's also difficult to be the parent who desires both on-field and off-field success for their child. There is anxiety in hoping that your son or daughter succeeds, and mounting pressure in our culture to make the car rides to and from practices full of critiques and lofty aspirations. We will help you understand a bit more about coaching and how parents can be supportive to their kids. We will share ideas as to what a well-rounded, satisfying player experience can look like (even if the team goes 1-12).

The end goal of this book, regardless of the reader, is to *describe the catalytic coaching behaviors necessary for parent-coaches to serve as positive role models for the kids.*

REMINDERS FROM YOUR CHILD

- I'm a **kid**.

- It's just a **game**.

- My coach is a **volunteer**.

- The officials are **human**.

- **No** college **scholarships** will be handed out today!

Becoming a Catalytic Coach

In 2018, one of our co-authors, Jerry Toomer, published a book entitled *The Catalyst Effect: 12 Skills and Behaviors to Boost Your Impact and Elevate Team Performance.* It described how certain individuals on all types of teams raised the performance of others when they were present.

The field research underlying the book addressed the core question: "Who do you know, that when they step onto the field or the court, into the conference room, or onto the stage, make others around them better?"

Leaders don't always require formal titles to be successful, and in fact, teams that allow individuals to "lead from wherever they are," * often see more powerful results. *The Catalyst Effect* studied these types of leaders in business, sports, and the arts and determined that several traits and characteristics were common among them. This produced a framework that can be applied to a wide variety of settings including youth sports teams.

The framework features skills in four key categories:

- Building Credibility and Establishing Trust

- Creating Cohesiveness and Positive Teamwork

---

* Copyrighted by The Catalyst Effect, Emerald Publishing, 2018.

- Generating Momentum: Sparking Enthusiasm and Developing Skills

- Amplifying Impact: Getting Positive Results for Kids, the Team, and Parents

This book for coaches blends research, real-world examples, and the catalytic framework to create a roadmap for those who want to teach players the soft skills that are so important to success on the field as well as later in life.

INPUT FROM THE COACHES SURVEY

We asked coaches in our field survey about their philosophy of coaching. The words that emerged as the most important were "fun" and "teach." Those are two foundational words to build around.

In this guide, we are incorporating perspectives we gleaned from approximately 200 coaches across the United States. These coaches represented a variety of sports and experience.

We conducted an online survey that was sent to coaching and league contacts. (Note: see more summary information about the survey in the Overtime section of this book.) We also conducted in-depth interviews, some with world-class youth coaches. Thanks to these coaches, we have been able to highlight the core beliefs, actions, and challenges that they face, and that we can now share with you.

What Does a Catalytic Coach Look Like?

When you ask yourself this question: "Who do you know that, when they step onto the field, onto the court, or into the conference room, make everyone around them better," and how do you describe these individuals?

The answer we heard most often was that they have a *catalytic impact* in that they spark excellence in others and positively impact the performance of the team. The Catalyst Effect model identifies the behaviors and skills needed to have that impact regardless of the team members *role* or *title*. You don't need to be the captain of the team or the most skilled player to have an immediate and lasting impact on others.

The Catalytic Effect model and the research behind it was, in part, the impetus for this coaching guide. Why? Because as we talked with athletes and coaches who described catalytic behaviors we realized that they are specific, definable, and trainable. We wanted to share our learning with coaches who can benefit from understanding how they can teach the soft skills to kids on their teams, i.e. *how to knowledgeably and intentionally teach these skills.*

A well-known example of a catalytic athlete is Shane Battier, college basketball player of the year at Duke University, college basketball Hall of Fame inductee, and a highly successful NBA player with the Grizzlies, Rockets, and Heat. In an article written by Michael Lewis in 2010, Battier was described as "The No Stats All Star." He was not regularly in the summary statistics as scoring the most points or getting the most rebounds, but "when he was on the court" the team played better. He was a positive catalyst.

Similarly, in soccer Christie Rampone was the reliable defender who spent eight years as the captain of the US national team, winning two Olympic golds and the 2015 World Cup during that stretch. "Internally for us she was the glue," coach Jill Ellis said in 2017. "She welcomed new players; she was a good communicator. She led by example but was also a strong leader within our group."*

The chapters that follow will briefly describe each set of skills, their associated behaviors, and will provide ideas as to how to teach each of these soft skills through examples and exercises.

So, ask yourself an additional question as you finish this chapter: Who was the "catalyst" in the baseball story that opened this chapter? And why? Our view is that the coach was a catalyst in that situation because he maintained a positive learning environment for the young players even amidst a series of losses.

How can you be a positive, catalytic influence in whatever coaching situation you find yourself?

---

* https://www.app.com/story/sports/2017/03/04/
edelson-christie-rampone-ceremony/98737132/

CHAPTER 2

Understanding Kids and Coaching

*"With younger kids, it's about having fun.
That does not necessarily mean accepting
mediocrity—that's simply the right approach
to help them enjoy what they're doing. Over
time, if the kids love the game, they will
have a desire to get better." –Scott Rush*

This guide is aimed at those coaches who work with some of our youngest athletes–ages 6 to 12. Anyone who has worked with children, raised them as parents, or frankly, even just observed them from afar, knows that a tremendous amount of cognitive, emotional, and physical development is happening with these young people. Sports is one part of their life, but so much more is happening around these experiences whether on the field, on the mat, on the court, in the pool, etc. They are exploring friendships–including the added element of how to manage friendships in the face of competition. They are learning how to interact with adults who are not their parents, for instance: teachers, church leaders, youth club advisors, the neighbor whose rose bush their cleats just trampled. They are also learning how to use their bodies. They become more aware of their physical capabilities.

Overall, when you are 6 to 12, you are trying to figure out what the heck is going on in your environment. Oh, and you're a kid. So, you're also trying to have fun!

What are Kids Thinking?!

So, now you're a coach to a sea of active bodies, minds, imaginations, and emotions. Can you teach them how to field a ground ball *and* encourage a teammate who just missed theirs? Can you teach them how to make an opposite-hand layup *and* be resilient when called for a foul? Of course, you can. That's part of what being a coach means. But it might help to understand a bit more about what they are thinking and feeling at those ages.

This time in a child's life is often referred to as *middle childhood*, and it's an amazing period of transition. As school tasks and expectations increase, these children need to call upon a number of mental processes to be successful–sequencing, understanding time, attentiveness, and memory recall. All of these are needed for success in sports as well, but effective coaches need to understand that these processes can be completely new or in the process of developing. For example, many baseball or softball coaches can find it frustrating that players take the field without their hat or forget their spot in the batting order. The truth is, their cognitive development is still catching up to such seemingly simple things. This is why patience can be a *key virtue* for coaches.

Socially, a young person in middle childhood is experiencing some major changes. Obviously a 6-year-old and a 12-year-old will have different experiences, but in general there are a few factors that tend to be shared.

Self-esteem and social acceptance are shared traits for those in middle childhood. A single day can feel like a roller coaster: success vs. failure, popularity vs. loneliness, calmness vs. stress, and so forth. Compounding self-esteem issues is the struggle to be accepted socially, to be in the "popular crowd." Nothing may sting more at this time of life than to feel isolated. All of this affects sense of self. Throughout middle childhood, youth may grow in their awareness of their weaknesses and strengths. A 6-year-old who struggles to dribble may still believe he should be a point guard. A 12-year-old who still struggles to dribble may accept that it's best for him to post-up instead. Middle childhood is also when youth become very modest about their bodies and compare their bodies to others. The same is true for athletic ability.

In the younger stages of middle childhood, identifying role models becomes important. Young people may seek to imitate adults in their lives (including you, coach!). In later stages, that shifts to peers and older kids. Young people become more observant of the different ways people act and are prone to copy those they see as cool.

With an established sense of self, those on the older side of middle childhood test their independence making them more willing to push back against adult authority.

IT'S NOT EASY BEING GREEN

It is not easy being a kid. It is normal for kids to have emotions that feel much bigger than they are, to feel them day in and day out and not really know how to process them. You may have heard that the part of a child's brain that rationally regulates emotions doesn't fully mature till they are in their 20s (yes, really!).

So, clearly a lot is going on. How do you make sense of all of this as a coach? The truth is, there is no magic formula. Every child is unique and may experience the factors described above differently. But to understand all of this is to acknowledge that coaching youth is a special skill set. It's not the same as managing your employees at the office or dealing with friends your age.

Your expectations should meet the developmental level of the ages you are working with. Simply keeping these factors in mind can prepare you to be more successful in your coaching role.

Here are some other considerations:

- According to thewholechild.org, A 6-year-old normally can follow a series of 3 commands in a row, and by age 10 most children can follow 5 commands in a row. Keep your instructions simple.

- Children at these ages can be very possessive of their belongings. Organize your practices so that each child's equipment has a place and it's easy for them to find.

- Attention spans are fleeting, especially for younger ages. Develop a call-and-response method to get attention. One of the authors observed his son's coach effectively, say "1-2-3 eyes on me" and they responded "1-2 eyes on you."

- In this age range, kids shift cognitively to more concrete thinking. So, heavily use demonstrations to get your point across.

Let's Talk about Coaching

Now that we have a better understanding of what goes on in the brains of youth in middle childhood, let's try to reach a better understanding of what coaching is. It is a more complicated role than most would give it credit for. Coaching is closely related to teaching. Here is a definition that we can use for the purposes of this book: *Coaching is experiential teaching, using acts of sport to help a learner grow in their physical, cognitive, and social-emotional abilities.*

Let's break it down:

Experiential: Coaching is based in helping a person achieve in an active setting and using the defined context of a sporting activity. The sport is the experience, and the coach is guiding a learner through their interaction with that experience. For example, you can't coach a person how to swim by handing them a book on swimming. They need to actually get in the pool, and when they try it is when the real learning occurs.

Coaching relates strongly to David Kolb's experiential learning cycle, which is an often-used framework in leadership development programs.

Concrete Experience
(doing / having an experience)

Active Experimentation
(planning / trying out what you have learned)

Reflective Observation
(reviewing / reflecting on the experience)

Abstract Conceptualization
(concluding / learning from the experience)

Using this model, let's consider a gymnast. A coach may pre-set the concrete experience by describing to the athlete what the balance beam is, and some tips for how to succeed on it. Nothing can really make sense until the athlete steps on the balance beam (concrete experience). The young athlete will likely fall off. It's in that moment the coach helps her consider why that happened (reflective observation). The athlete will consider what happened and think through how to avoid falling off again, including what helps her achieve a good sense of balance (abstract conceptualization). She will then try out this new learning (active experimentation), get back on the beam and the cycle repeats.

A coach could handle this a few different ways, which is what can make coaching philosophies and styles unique. A forceful, command and control coach, might shout and instruct the athlete while they are on the beam. A highly relaxed, laissez-faire coach might not say anything at all, and let the athlete process on her own. And then there is a continuum of options between these. Kolb's model looks friendlier among those who are less commanding, and instead can use questions and helpful prodding to get an athlete to make sense of her experience on her own.

The Act of sport: While coaching has become a generalized term that could include personalized mentorship from a consultant to a professional, we're staying pretty tight in this guide to its traditional use as a term in sports. Although, many of the lessons in this guide can be transferable to other settings and relationships.

Help a learner: Maybe a small change in terminology can help you see your role as a coach with a little more importance. You can see the kids in front of you as simply kids or players. Or you can see them as learners. If they are learning, then you are indeed teaching, and the experience is truly one that transcends the win-loss record or a score.

Grow in their physical, cognitive, and social-emotional abilities: This is obviously key, and where the coaching role gets the most complicated. Sports is an excellent context to learn many things beyond the rules of a particular game and the skills for how to execute that game. It is also a context for problem-solving, forecasting, diagramming, and other cognitive abilities. Sports also provide a wonderful venue for individuals to learn confidence, kindness, listening, and other social-emotional capacities. Because of this broad educational context, effective coaching can support growth in all of these areas, especially with young children. If that feels like a lot of pressure, that's a valid feeling. This guide is meant to help ease that pressure and provide practical tools that can help you be successful.

POSITIVE FACTORS OF BRAIN DEVELOPMENT

Health

- Exercise increases the flow of blood to the brain.

- It's very good for the brain because it increases heart rate, which pumps more oxygen to the brain.

- Exercise makes it easier for children to learn. It makes the information in their mind to be fresh and helps the child have a better understanding.

- The brain is actively undergoing synaptic pruning and, as such, is constantly becoming more refined, a process that is heavily dependent on a child's environment.

- Exercise stimulates the brain's plasticity by stimulating growth of new connections between cells in a wide array of important cortical areas of the brain.

- It is demonstrated that exercise increased growth factors in the brain, making it easier for the brain to grow new neuronal connections.

The definition of coaching we are using above is a baseline (the coach is guiding a learner through their interaction with that experience.). The philosophy you bring to the act of coaching is what will give it life. The same is true in leadership. We may all understand what a leader is, but yet there can be authoritarian leaders, servant leaders, visionary leaders, quiet leaders, and so on. All are models for leading and for helping others learn, but each approach has its own unique characteristics—and varying levels of effectiveness.

Who are You as a Coach?

What behaviors do you model for the kids, your co-coaches, and the parents? You can be a commanding coach. Or you can be an exceptionally supportive and caring coach. What we propose, based on research for this book and prior research from *The Catalyst Effect*, is that in order to maximize your effectiveness as a coach, you should strive to be a *Catalytic Coach*. This is a coach ***who tries to make everyone around him or her better and thereby inspires them to do the same.***

You raised your hand to volunteer to be a coach, or you were talked into coaching by a league organizer or your spouse or a friend! Of course, most of you won't see coaching as your primary vocation. So, we want to provide you with specific suggestions and tools that can make coaching easier and more enjoyable.

The most effective youth sports coaches want the experience to be *fun for the kids*. It should be fun and enjoyable for you too. If it's not fun, you and your coaching team should do some self-reflection. This guide will hopefully lower your stress level and help you build confidence. The most effective coaches indicate that caring matters. If you care about this role, and strive to do your best, most everything else will fall into place.

What Is Your Coaching Philosophy?

Do you even have a coaching philosophy? Maybe so, but perhaps it is not clearly articulated? What would you tell the parents of your players about your coaching style and the outcomes you seek from using that style? We advocate strongly for having a thoughtful coaching philosophy that can be the foundation for when the peaks and valleys of a season take their toll.

Scott Rush is a baseball coach who took his team, Maine-Endwell Little League, to the Little League World Series in 2011. So, he's a very accomplished coach and far from being a beginner. What might surprise you about Scott is that his coaching philosophy is not a "win at all costs" approach. He has had success, yes, but that success is grounded in key principles that would be useful at any level and with any team. He shared four key principles with us:

1. Players should have fun and their experience should be positive.

2. Players should learn to love the game.

3. Players should be inspired not to win, but to be competitive.

4. The coach's job is to help them learn and develop.

"FUN" IS CENTRAL IS SUCCESSFUL EXPERIENCES FOR OUR KIDS.

To help you think about writing your approach to coaching, consider the words that emerged most frequently when the coaches in our survey revealed their philosophies: fun, team, teach, learn. (Note: see more detail in the Overtime section of the book.) These terms were most frequently mentioned no matter how many years of experience the coaches had. Thus, the first-year, first-time parent coach and the long-time seasoned coach all put "fun," "team," "teach," and "learn" front and center.

Fun also popped off the page when we analyzed the adjectives our coaches wanted their players to use for them. According to our coaches, greater than the desire to see their players hold up a gold-plastic championship trophy was the desire to hear them say, "I had fun, coach!"

One of the most central takeaways from the survey and interviews we conducted was this:

What is most important is for the kids to have fun and develop a love for the game.

Jay Baker is a coach in a Little League baseball program in Zionsville, Indiana (minutes North of

Indianapolis). Jay has been long considered in his community as someone kids want to play for and who parents hope is assigned to their child's team. Jay has a lot of the qualities that make him caring: approachable, calm, and pleasant to be around. He also recognizes that fun is paramount. One drill that Jay uses for his youth baseball teams is meant to help the players learn to track a fly ball heading into the outfield.

Many younger players have difficulty seeing where the ball is heading–either left or right, or in front of them or over their head. This leaves them to either stand still and watch the ball land or run in circles trying to judge the ball's trajectory. During practice, Jay will have the players put on their batting helmets and gloves and go to the outfield. One at a time, Jay will loft a tennis ball into the air and each player's goal is to get the ball to hit them on top of their helmet-protected head. You can imagine that kids find this hilarious (likely also the adults watching), and it produces laughter and cheers. Jay will also award bonus points to the kids that can catch the ball off the head-bounce with their glove. The idea is to help them position their bodies in the right place to make the play, and it's an innovative and fun way to accomplish the lesson.

Below are several questions to consider when you are thinking through your coaching philosophy.

Answering these could help you synthesize your thoughts into a coherent coaching approach.

1. How will you describe to parents the way you coach? In written form? In a parent meeting?

2. What do you expect from parents? Do you want them to be hands-on with volunteering, or stay in the stands?

3. How will you communicate expectations to the players at the beginning of the season?

4. What will you do when one of your players makes a mistake? What if it's a game-deciding mistake?

5. What types of players do you think you'll more naturally click with? Which type would be the opposite? How will you adapt your style to different players?

6. How do you prefer to receive constructive input (or complaints) from players and parents?

7. What might your pre-game comments include?

8. What do your post-game comments focus on?

Here's a sample email to parents and players for you to consider.

GREETINGS TEAM TOGO FAMILIES!

We are excited for another season of soccer and are pleased to have your kiddos on the team. Let's have some fun.

This will be the third season of coaching for Coach K (Kurtis), Coach Beau, and me. We continue to come back (as do our children) because we believe in the NESA mission and its focus on community, which leads to a great atmosphere and style of play. More than that, we have the privilege of helping to develop good athletes *and* good teammates!

As you know from league registration, the parent code of conduct outlines the agreements which ensure we all do our part to fulfill the league mission. Thank you for your support. With input from our players, we will discuss team expectations, which are likely to include themes around being a good teammate, giving one's best effort, treating others with respect, bouncing back when something goes wrong, and of course, having fun! Our "team rules" help us stay on track and in step with the spirit of the league.

We will do our best to make practices and games meaningful and full of growth opportunities. Further, it is our goal to ensure that playing time is distributed as fairly as possible while balancing odd numbers and game circumstances. Please feel free to contact any one of us with questions or concerns if they arise during the course of the season.

Oh, and the snacks! This may be THE highlight of each Saturday morning for our team. At our first practice, I will have a signup sheet to ensure our game days covered. We look forward to seeing you all next week.

Thank you, and Go Team Togo!

CHAPTER 3

Building Credibility and Establishing Trust

"Earn trust, earn trust, earn trust.
Then you can worry about
the rest." –Seth Godin

Mindy O. spent several years watching her husband coach their oldest son's sports teams. When
it came time for her youngest to start tee-ball, the
league needed a coach and her husband couldn't
take it on. Mindy answered the call so that there
could be a team. "I couldn't be further from what
a coach would look like," she recalled. But, she
was always up for a challenge and decided to try.
Turns out, Mindy became an excellent (and now
sought-after) tee-ball coach despite not having
any experience and admittedly little knowledge
of drills and skills. Why? "I focused a lot on teaching them to be positive and supportive with each
other. When mistakes happened, I would take

time to talk to them personally. A lot of it is listening to them to find out how they're feeling." This simple but effective formula is a good example of a coach **building credibility**.

What does building credibility as a coach mean to you?

Building credibility is the "price of admission" to being a great catalyst on a team or a great coach. To build credibility, these key skills need to be present: *trust, communication and listening, and optimism*. These are foundational to both coaching and team success–without them, mastering the more advanced skills effectively will be difficult.

CREDIBILITY IS A COACH'S BEST FRIEND

One of the key skills of the *Catalyst Effect* is the importance of Building Credibility. The coaches we surveyed repeatedly stated that this is the most important cornerstone for coaching youth sports as well! Don Showalter, USA Basketball Executive and coach, believes that building relationships with players is the highest priority because then they trust you and become more coachable.

In fact, as part of the survey, we invited coaches to evaluate several statements with regard to how important they are for a youth sports coach to be successful. Six out of the top ten statements could be assigned to the idea of credibility:

- *Acting with Integrity/Building trust with team.*

- *Communicating clearly to players.*

- *Showing your players that you Care about them.*

- *Teaching that failure is an opportunity to Learn.*

- *Viewing the game with Optimism and sharing this outlook with the team.*

- *Being Passionate about developing youth.*

Consistent with our survey findings, The Search Institute, a youth development research organization in Minneapolis, describes 40 development assets that are important for young people to have in order to grow into healthy and productive adults. Many of these assets can be revealed in youth sports, particularly one that states that youth should have supportive relationships with three or more adults in addition to their parents or guardians. The Search Institute's research shows that young people who experience this support feel happier and more hopeful, do better in school, and are less likely to rely on destructive behaviors (such as drugs) in order to fit in. A young person's coach, the male or female adult figure who runs their practices and is present as they execute on the playing field, can be one of these non-parent adults. However, without credibility this relationship doesn't fully bloom, and have the social and behavioral impact it should. If the young person isn't feeling authentically cared for or trusted, then the relationship will suffer.

Trust

To build trust and commitment as a coach and for her players alike, an elite volleyball coach asks her players to do three very simple things when they are practicing:

1. Show up 5 minutes early for practice (and be "ready to play" at the start time),

2. Stand on their spot in the circle around the coach in a respectful manner, and

3. Run with *enthusiasm and focus* to and from the drills she asks them to complete.

These are simple and quite powerful. First, show up! Parent and kids are encouraged to be *ready to play* at X:00; not running from the car to the field or court with shoes and bag in hand, but *ready to play*. This also means that the coaches are there early and have everything ready to go. As a coach give yourself 15 minutes for set up before the team arrives–it builds confidence and trust in *your* preparation and commitment.

Communication

We could argue that the most important skill of all in being a successful coach is clearly sending messages and information to the players, *and* listening to them in a comfortable, relaxed manner.

> "I'd say handling people is the most important thing you can do as a coach. I've found every time I've

gotten into trouble with a player, it's because I wasn't talking to him enough."

Lou Holtz, Former American Football Player, Coach, and Analyst

Much of what we describe in this guide is in some way connected to or based on clear communication.

In a previous chapter, we discussed what kids at these ages hear, what their attention span is, and how complex or simple the messages need to be. With that in mind, and realizing that most of us adults tend to talk more than our kids have the capacity to absorb, coaches must *work to keep messages crisp, clear, and simple and repeat them to ensure understanding.*

Be clear about the *one or two key* messages you are sending. Simplify for your audience. This is often harder than it seems, especially if you have been communicating more complex ideas in a work setting with adults all day.

Listening

Mindy's story of success as a first-time coach came from her willingness to listen. Of course, at these ages, non-verbal cues are key. When possible, move physically to the kids' level. Kneel, sit down, take a non-threatening posture and position that invites them to connect with you via eyes and ears. You are likely big, and potentially imposing, in their eyes. A dad or mom with clipboard, whistle, hat, and an authoritative look can inspire discipline, yes, but may limit the number of honest questions or the full engagement that we want to build with our players.

When do you take a player aside and talk with them individually? Do you build coach/player chats into your coaching routine from the beginning? Do they have goals for the season that you can support? Do they have concerns or anxieties that you can understand and help them to mitigate? (Note: given most league guidelines regarding adult-child interactions, it is very important that another coach or adult be present.)

For some coaches, this individual discussion excites them and comes easily–they want to connect with each kid on a personal level. For others, this might push you out of your comfort zone. If it's a challenge, perhaps that's where a skilled assistant coach can help you.

At age 7, this may be a different experience than say age 11. In any case be clear about what you want to accomplish in addition to building trust and listening to what their individual goals or concerns are. This simple conversation may go a long, long way in gaining their engagement with you and the team. And, you can consider foreshadowing this conversation in your introductory email to parents and kids as the season begins, as we mentioned in the prior chapter with Team Togo.

DO I COMMUNICATE WELL WITH KIDS AT THESE AGES?

In our survey of coaches, a few beliefs showed much stronger emphasis than others, and those mostly related to effective communication. For example, when asked if speaking or listening is more important as a coach, **listening was the clear winner**. It's noteworthy to mention that those same coaches admitted in their actions they often rely on speaking more than listening. However, armed with a belief that the players should be heard and acknowledged, these coaches were more likely to be successful in stopping to truly listen to their player's needs and wants.

Also in line with effective communication was the belief of most coaches we surveyed that if a player doesn't comprehend a particular point or lesson, it was the coach's responsibility to more clearly communicate the lesson. This may seem pretty basic, but it's a clear indicator of a coach's role as educator. In a classroom environment, if a student can't report back learning on a particular lesson, piece of information, or new knowledge, a teacher isn't likely to throw up his or her hands and blame the student. Similarly, if a player is not understanding a particular technique or play in basketball, for example, effective coaches will stop and ensure it is explained better or differently so that the player can be successful.

A third belief from the survey that highlights the importance of communication is the role of feedback. By a large margin, the coaches in our survey believe (and also practice) the idea that providing positive feedback is more important and effective than giving critical feedback. This could change as players get older and competition gets harder, but in youth sports it appears that players want to understand what they're doing well and have emphasis placed on that. The coaches in our survey are willing to meet them there.

Don Showalter advises:

When you see the bigger picture, you're going to use some of these soft skills. If you're just trying to win, you don't care about these skills. If I'm a coach who cares about my players' development, I'll care about the things that make them a great teammate. Such as: give credit, help someone up if they fall, or give two people a high five. Develop that teamwork and build communication. Develop the notion that being a great teammate is important. For instance, clap for your teammate when he comes back to the bench.

To develop trust as a coach, you do what you say – follow through. If you tell a teammate he's going to play 10 minutes, then make sure he plays 10 minutes. In practice session, the winner gets a pair of socks. (These kids love socks!) If you never give them to him, he's lost all trust in you. Trust and humility need to be demonstrated to the players.

In a practice, we add communications into it. We have a Communication Circle at the end of every practice where we circle up and hold hands and have a question for the day, it might be to <u>tell</u> the player beside you what they did well in practice. "Marty, you did a great job of rebounding…" And we go around the circle that way. Players understand their roles this way, and understand that not every player has the same role. This gives the players motivation to become skilled at a different role. It's a great way to communicate and makes players understand what you need to do to be a great teammate and what other teammates need to do as well.

Optimism

The book, *The Catalyst Effect,* describes a high performing McDonald's restaurant at which the "sparkplug" or the catalyst for optimism on the team was obvious to everyone. Angie's behaviors included: offering a positive word to others ("nice job" or "way to go"), asking them how they are doing or feeling, making the effort to smile and connect with each person directly, demonstrating a "can do" attitude by volunteering for new jobs (or drills!).

This overall attitude of optimism and a "can do"

spirit on the part of the coaches cannot be over-emphasized. As with author's example of his 1-12 baseball team at the beginning of the book, even in the face of relatively few wins and marginal team success, the coaches can remain committed to having fun with the kids and recognizing the positives at every turn. We don't wallow in our mistakes–we learn from them and move forward.

AM I AN APPROACHABLE COACH?

As mentioned before, coaches want to be described as fun. Interestingly, the other adjectives that were mentioned most frequently in the survey stayed consistent with that theme, instead of drifting more towards the caricature of the tough and mean coach that always pushes hard. The coaches we studied, no matter their level of experience, type of sport, gender, or any other factor used these powerful words most of all: *caring, encouraging, passionate, fair, and positive.* This mirrors a societal trend towards servant leadership and emotional intelligence, and might be the words we'd use to describe an ideal boss or teacher.

When asked to consider coaches they admire and the qualities that come to mind, the survey respondents shared many of the same social-emotional terms: *caring, teaching, knowledgeable, positive, and patient.*

What is emerging from these responses

is the picture of a coach that is approachable, other-centered, and who is a patient educator.

More Mr. Miyagi and less Cobra Kai (Karate Kid).

John, one of our authors, was once an assistant on a team that was struggling, and the head coach had a particular knack for making kids laugh and enjoy themselves in spite of it. For example, the kids might have a rough inning in the field with errors and several runs scored, and when it was mercifully over he would call them over to do a cheer before they grabbed their bats for their turn to hit. Instead of the traditional cheer of "hits!" or "runs!", this coach would have them shout something ridiculous, like "Wedgie!" or "Batman!" Within the smiles and chuckles that came from the kids was also a letting-go of the struggles they just lived through. *It's a good reminder that kids can be resilient, especially when given a chance to just be kids.*

You might ask yourself:

- How do you wish to be viewed by the kids that you coach? By their parents?

- How can you intentionally establish expectations at the beginning of the season that layout the way you will coach...and be viewed as a coach?

- Is it natural for you to be casual, fun-loving? Or are more serious and focused on team skills or wins? How can you find the proper balance for you, the kids, the parents?

- Have you talked with your assistant coaches about being consistent with the kids in terms of how you communicate with them, and what you expect from them? As a group of coaches, do you agree on your approach?

CHAPTER 4

Creating Cohesion and Positive Teamwork

"Earn your leadership every day." –Michael Jordan

Imagine you are on a highly competitive basketball team, where every second of practice is valuable for getting every detail right. But yet, several of those seconds–minutes actually–are spent standing in a circle with your teammates and coaches holding hands. Each person in the circle is expected to give positive feedback to someone else in the circle. You will likely do this again tomorrow at the end of practice, but with a different question to respond to.

Why would a successful team sacrifice valuable minutes on the court this way?
According to longtime basketball coach, Don Showalter, it's to build team unity. Don has

coached for 42 years, and has come to understand the power of cohesion for team success. Taking these moments to share a positive thought with a teammate, and receive one in kind, builds camaraderie, emphasizes the unique contributions each player brings, and builds tighter connections.

Don wants players who give credit away, help others up from the floor, constantly give high-fives, and always clap for teammates when they come back to the bench.

What Does Teamwork Mean to Your Players?

Kids on teams have common goals: to enjoy the experience, develop skills, make friends, and hopefully experience winning—and losing some games. If you have drafted your "approach to coaching" comments, as suggested in Chapter 2, you have given some thought to what is important to you as you work with the kids. Your comments likely include the idea of teamwork. "How can you help the kids understand how to balance their individual concerns and goals with those of the team as a whole?" This section will provide you with some suggestions as to how to convey those ideas effectively.

WAYS TO EMPHASIZE COMMITMENT TO THE TEAM

As a reminder and related suggestion, do you draft and send a pre-season note to parents?

(See Team Togo example in Chapter 2.) This note may include your approach to coaching and include how you and parents can work together to help kids understand that team goals come first. Kids at this age are focused on self: how do I look, how good am I compared to my friends, will I embarrass myself, does my coach treat me fairly? The parents are similarly concerned, in many instances, as to how their kids present themselves… and how that reflects on their family and them as parents. Therefore, emphasizing the team, and each player's commitment to the team, is key.

What is Cohesiveness and Positive Teamwork?

Cohesiveness is the extent to which team members stick together and remain united in the pursuit of a common goal. The relationships that bind young players on the team together are key to success. Without cohesiveness and a sense of "we-ness," the team may be fragmented by individual goals that players have (or that parents have for their kids).

So even though each member of a team will have individual aspirations, it's important for a coach to set the tone for overall team goals. The coach needs to emphasize that: *We succeed and grow together and we win or lose as a team.*

What is your team's identity? What is your motto or shared language that the team can rally around? For instance, one of the authors is connected to a successful youth baseball coach that has six rules that help shape the identity of the team and serve as a verbal contract.

The rules are:

1. Golden Rule: Be a great teammate and treat others the way you want to be treated.

2. Have Fun.

3. Always try your best.

4. When a coach is talking, you are listening.

5. Keep the ball in front of you.

6. Play quicker–bat swing, base running, defense.

The coach is able to then hold the players accountable by referring to the number of the rule. If a player is being a bit rowdy, for example, he says: "Tommy, rule #4." If a player is lazy in their attempt to field a ball, the coach (and maybe the other players) are quick to point out "rule #3!" The coach emphasizes these in each practice, asking the team to recite them at times. For kids at this age, having six core ideas to rally behind is enough.

Talking with Your Team

What are the straightforward discussions you can have with your team about working together? For instance, similar to the example at the start of this chapter, have the kids form a circle at the beginning of a practice, ask them each for one word that describes what success looks like as a team for this season.

Always provide an opportunity for them to "pass," and feel free to go around a second time if you are looking for more adjectives that get at the ideas of "team" and "cohesiveness." Include your assistant coaches and yourself in the circle to help ensure that you are getting the type of input that speaks to "we-ness." Creating a safe space and a place for these conversations is essential to being an effective coach of young athletes.

It's a good sign if you hear words or phrases from the kids that include: respecting others, trying our best, talking nicely to each other, helping each other, being humble when we win, admitting our mistakes, celebrating together, having fun, or learning more about how to play better.

Consider repeating this discussion mid-season and post-season. Ask yourselves, did we accomplish what we set out to do? Did we not only accomplish the straightforward team goals of winning some games or finishing first, but did we also learn how to play together and learn together as good teammates?

You can recognize certain kids as positive contributors, or catalysts, to teamwork. For instance, these may be kids who were not the stars of the team: "I was really happy to see Kris help the other player get back on her feet." Or, you can choose to describe the overall actions and behavior of several kids that made the team better:

- "I was happy to see you all rally around a teammate when she was hurt in the game last week."

- "Did you notice how nice it was that our team was very respectful in our post-game line up with the other team? Even though some of their kids wouldn't shake hands, I was proud that each of you stayed focused on being polite and achieving our goal of being a group of respectful players."

Never hesitate to share your pride and enthusiasm for what the team has accomplished. As a coach, you play an important role in helping players identify *both* the individual and team goals they wish to achieve.

Questions:

- Do you talk with each of the kids on your team about how to be a good teammate?

- Do you talk with the team as a whole about what they would like to accomplish as a team?

- Do you set the example for the kids on what a good teammate looks like?

- Are you establishing a team identity anchored to a set of rules?

- Do you have a team language or rallying cry that binds the team together? "We are Team Togo!"

CHAPTER 5

Generating Momentum: Sparking Enthusiasm and Developing Skills

"When we give ourselves permission to fail, we, at the same time, give ourselves permission to excel." – Eloise Ristad

For John's 1-12 baseball team example earlier in the book, momentum was not on his side. They could not rely on successes that would help them optimistically push forward. How could they celebrate the positives and wins when they didn't exist? How could he find the momentum in the midst of team losses? This can be stressful to a coach because we all want the kids to enjoy their experience and be proud of their accomplishments.

Momentum is key to progress for teams and individuals. In sports, it's often referred to as the "big Mo" factor. Teams that get on a run, continue to build on the enthusiasm that comes with success.

They are *in a zone* and feed off of each other's positive energy.

We have no magic wand here, but there are some specific concepts that might make sense to you.

First, consider viewing building momentum as an individual concept, as well as a team phenomenon. Each of your players has a certain level of engagement and energy when they come to practice or to a game or match. You can influence that as a coach. Without overwhelming them with your adult energy, you do play a key role in bringing your enthusiasm to the team. Even in the midst of a series of losses, you can choose to bring an optimistic presence to the team. You and your fellow coaches set the tone from the outset of practice–the bounce in your step, visible excitement about the practice you are about to have, or the simple introductory comments you make about getting better today.

Note: if you've had a series of losses or a particularly tough loss, it's not about *you* and your possible feelings of failure as a coach, it's about igniting or re-igniting the enthusiasm of the kids. One of the authors confessed to having had a less than positive experience with his personal emotions. He was so upset with a team loss that he left at the end of the game without speaking to the team or the parents. Only later did he realize, regretfully, that it was not about him. He felt disappointed that he had not been supportive of his team's effort and shared those feelings with them at the next practice.

Coaches are human. We make mistakes. We can

share appropriate apologies or regret with our players because it is a real part of life and learning.

One key factor to keep in mind is that the rewards that motivate or ignite enthusiasm in kids might be substantially different than for adults. During the stretch of losses, John found he could create a little boost of momentum by surprising the kids with popsicles at the end of practice. (One of the coaches we interviewed gave the kids socks – apparently his team loved them!) Do you have several ideas in your bag of coaching tricks as to how to boost momentum?

Although not as flavorful as popsicles, an important technique is to remind kids of their individual goals and growth. Momentum can be about *improvement*, not just wins and losses. Once you get to know the kids a bit, we suggest that you set goals with each player near the beginning of the season. For some of the older kids, consider *two goals* for each player: one in the technical skill area and another in the soft skill or interpersonal area.

Catalytic coaches reinforce the step-by-step progress each player makes. They celebrate accomplishments and improvements–step-by-step; bit-by-bit. They help kids to recognize and embrace successes *during* each practice or game so they leave the field, court, gym, or pool feeling positive.

For example, Maria (age 10) had set two goals with her soccer coach:

1. Improve her ball control while dribbling.

2. Keep her spirits up even when she made a mistake on the field (don't get too self-critical).

The first goal was straightforward. Understanding how to use her feet to keep the ball in a controlled space in front of her and how to keep the ball relatively close while keeping it from getting away from her was physically clear to her and her coach. Practicing dribbling drills around the orange cones helped her make progress, as did practice at home with her sister and mom during the week. She asked if she could borrow a couple of cones to practice with at home and of course the answer was "yes" (but please bring them to practice next week). Her improvement over several practices was visible and was a direct result of her putting in the time, effort, and focus to make progress.

As a coach, recognizing her improvement in dribbling drills and expressing appreciation for her work in between formal practices helped her feel like she was making progress and that she was building individual momentum. And, it laid the foundation for her to continue to grow in other technical areas of the sport.

The second goal was also behaviorally clear even though it was a soft skill. When Maria made a bad pass in practice or games, she would slap her leg, hang her head, and mumble something to herself about her mistake. In doing that, it not only distracted from her play for the next couple of minutes, but it also impacted others on the team who observed her getting upset with herself. Maria and other players would lose momentum. The goal for Maria became to *keep her spirits up and hustle on to the next play.*

As her coach, the opportunity to note improvement in her positive behaviors (keeping her spirits up) is clearly identifiable and easy to comment on: "Maria, great job looking ahead to the next play, keeping your eyes up, and hustling across the field to back up Joleen." That can go a long way to building "Mo" for Maria's improvement and for igniting the rest of the team as well.

Should the young players share their development goals with their parents and the rest of the team? Sure! Why not? One coach we spoke with has his baseball players write three goals on an index card and then tape the card on a bathroom mirror so they see it daily. This coach also asked for photos of the goals, which he then shared with other parents and players, resulting in enhanced teambuilding and accountability. This builds the feeling of everyone working to improve and ideally the team members reinforcing one another along the way. To parents, the question can be: "What did my kid learn today?" Or "How did they make progress on the goal(s) that they set with coach?"

LEARNING NEVER ENDS

This learning process is continuous. Whether you are age two or fifty-two, the work of learning is never done! Whether a coach or player, your job is to learn continuously!

By the way, do you have goals for developing as a coach? How can you improve your coaching skills throughout the year? If you have personal goals, share them with your co-coaches and with the parents and kids. And, it's not a bad idea to tape them to your bathroom mirror!

Model the commitment to getting better as a coach and talk about your progress, or setbacks, with your team.

Learning New Skills

Remember Jay Baker from earlier in the book who we introduced as a player and parent-favorite Little League coach in a small town in Indiana?

In Little League, every kid wants to try pitching. But those who have watched these games know that there are some kids simply not cut out for that. One of Jay's strengths is his ability to use the art of managing expectations to help kids get that shot, but not negatively impact team performance. He would say "just give me five pitches." If the kid performs better than expected, he stays in, but if he struggles it is easy for Jay to say, "Thanks, you did what I asked you to do," and there is no major erosion of confidence. The player got to experience pitching and others could easily be supportive.

Developing a passion for learning at an early age is key to success in adolescence and adulthood.

Coaches have a unique opportunity to foster this confident attitude in the kids on their teams. When kids want to pitch, or play point guard, do you give them their shot even though success may not be likely? In most instances in recreational leagues, the answer is "yes." However, managing expectations may take the pressure off both the coach and the player. Jay was able to set expectations so that he could give them a shot at pitching without negatively impacting the team or embarrassing them. They got to try!

We learn through trying and failing, and many argue that's where the greatest lessons are found. Walking, riding a bike, doing a flip on the trampoline, shooting a free throw–we only learn through trying, failing, and trying again. Both physically and mentally, we build the muscles that underlie our hunger to learn, master a new skill, and build the confidence that we can do it again.

Consider the learning cycle that we shared in Chapter 2. Learning is dependent on the individual trying a new behavior, likely failing the first time, and then reflecting on how they might modify their approach the next time. The coach's role is to keep that experience light enough to be fun while pointing out how the player can develop mastery of the skills involved. The coach helps build that confidence and momentum. The process is straightforward:

- Describe and/or demonstrate the skill. For example, the most effective defensive position in basketball is with feet parallel, body low, weight able to be shifted easily in order to stay in front of the offensive player.

- The players try the skill. Perhaps they cross their feet or stand too upright. There are some positive things that they did and some room for improvement.

- The coach reflects on the positives of what they did and offers suggestions for improvement. "Your feet are parallel and in good position. Your body could be even lower to the ground, like this."

- The players try again.

- The coach recognizes progress and the small steps of improvement.

There is nothing highly complex about this cycle of learning. Confidence builds when there is a balance of "success and failure" so the kids feel like they are making progress, that there is a safe space to take risks, and that the coach validates what they are doing.

The coach can also demonstrate his or her own commitment to learning. It is powerful when the kids and parents see the coach talk about their own learning process. You can try out new things (perhaps demonstrating a drill in a way that is not so perfect!) or discuss what you have learned from another coach, or a video clip you watched, or a training session you attended.

Extract lessons learned and talk about them with the team. For instance, "Hey team, I learned something new that I want to show you!" Experimenting with new ideas, game plans, and practice drills as a coach builds a team culture of improvement for everyone involved, including you and your fellow coaches.

A LESSON FROM THE COACHES PLAYBOOK

Scott Rush told us:

> I talk to other coaches or watch them and use their techniques. I've learned in my professional career that I'm not the smartest one in the room so I have no problem looking at who on a coaching staff does something really well, then I pick up those techniques. I observed one coach who worked at the professional level and was on the World Series coaching team. I had the opportunity to bounce ideas around with him. From another coach (football), I learned how to handle crowds and media. It's important to leverage strengths of those around us and it's a good lesson for the kids. You

can't play all positions. You realize
that there are people who are pretty
smart and have good ideas. You need
to learn to make the most everyone
around you.

Bringing Energy and Focus

This idea is a bit difficult to describe. It is pretty straightforward to envision the highly active coaching staff running up and down the sidelines, verbally encouraging the kids, and being fully into the game. But it is not always pretty. The game can become more about the coach, or an "energized" parent, than the players.

An effective catalytic coach should bring their authentic personality to practices and games as you show enthusiasm in your own way. Let it be visible as you engage with players and parents as they arrive at practice. Greeting them by name could be the simplest yet the most powerful thing a coach does. If the kids are newer to you or each other, get name tags and put them on their shirts for the first couple of practices. (Quick tip, affix it to the back of their shirt since you spend so much time watching them in drills from behind). Let them know you are pleased to see them and that you are happy to be there with them.

As a team of coaches, assuming that you have more than one coach working with the kids, you can hopefully connect with each young player at each practice and game. This will help them feel that they are a key part of the team and that they have a positive opportunity to fully engage.

Another way to bring energy is to make decisions at practice participatory. Let the kids weigh in on decisions about practice time and drills when it makes sense. One way to avoid having to say no to their ideas is to give them two-to-three options, and let them decide and explain their decision. It teaches them how to work together on team decisions without the coach always telling them what to do.

"Give players a voice and a choice."
– Fritz Ettl, Butler University

Helping the kids focus on the energy that they bring to the game as players provides them with more responsibility and ownership of what they are doing on the court or the field.

Youth sports are about many things that can be enhanced with positive focus and energy: kids having fun, getting better at skills, working together as a team, and learning to make decisions on their own. Remind yourself as a coach that children can figure out where to pass a ball and when to take a shot without an adult telling them what to do <u>every</u> step of the way. *It's their game, not yours.*

Providing post-practice or post-game feedback is another way to emphasize this. At the end of practice or a game consider asking the team when you circle up: "What went well today?" "What could we have done better today?" "Do you want to recognize anyone who made a special contribution to practice?" Keep this short, energetic, and positive.

Leading and Following

Your star players can also be your best followers. Think about that for a moment. *When do you want your best players to also know how to follow others?*

Even at a young age, or perhaps *especially* at younger ages, there are kids who stand out as star players. They may be bigger, faster, more coordinated, and just more naturally athletic. Of course, to be successful as a coach and get some wins, you want to develop your most highly skilled players and use them strategically to help the team perform well. But here are two things to consider about star players.

First, being a star is not always about being the highest scorer or the most dominant player. A star may be the kid who "helps make others around them better." A useful consideration might be to remember Shane Battier, the No Stats All Star. Which players, when they are on the field or the court, tend to bring energy and skills that make others around them better?

Shane was not often in the box score highlights for most points or rebounds, but when the Houston Rockets analyzed their overall performance metrics, they found that when he was on the floor the team consistently performed better (see *The Catalyst Effect* for a full picture of these competencies). Battier led "from the middle" so to speak. He was a player that everyone wanted to have on the court with them. In hockey, this is often referred to as "plus-minus" as a way to think about players who add to the team's energy and performance versus those who subtract from it. So, the questions for coaches of younger players is similar: "Who are the kids who ignite the play of others?" "And, how can you deploy and recognize these players appropriately?"

Second, how can you encourage your star players, your most gifted athletes, to "follow" when needed? To step back and to accept a secondary role. One place to start is by pointing out that assists, strong defense, and ball distribution are often as important as points or goals scored. Some of these conversations may occur individually with the player along with you and your assistant coach. Intentionally providing recognition for stars when they follow and foster team play seamlessly can be highly valuable in their learning process–and more importantly, in their lives.

We know that working on project teams in future roles in their lives is an important part of many or most jobs. Helping kids understand how they can flexibly lead *or* follow at the right times in support of the mission and goals of a team is an attitude and skill set that will serve them well as adults.

Consider a very different setting: Improv. One fundamental skill of improv is to be able to both lead and follow. This is realized on stage as improv players alternate taking the lead and then following the lead of the other person(s). The short-hand term for this is "Yes….And…" Rather than changing the subject or rejecting what another person has introduced as a topic, the other player literally says "Yes…And…" rather than "No…But…" in a manner that validates the topic and then builds on it. Similarly, in music we see this play out in the improvisational jazz world.

Thinking back on this chapter, what are the key takeaways?

- How can you create a safe space where young players can try new behaviors and enhance learning? See an example later in Chapter 6 that describes how one youth coach communicates at the end of each season with a personal note to each player that focuses on how important it is for kids to learn, and to have fun doing it.

- How can you model behavior that indicates that you and your fellow coaches are learning as well? Do you write a personal note to your fellow coaches as well as to your players?

- Do you find regular ways to genuinely re-ward and reinforce learning along with good performance?

- How can you help young players understand that it is just as important to the team to be able to follow when needed as well as to lead?

CHAPTER 6

Amplifying Impact: Getting Positive Results for Kids, the Team, and Parents

"You miss 100% of the shots you don't take. –Wayne Gretzky

There we were again. My son, standing next to me in the dugout, in a winner-take-all game, both of us anxious for the outcome. It was a lopsided score. I thought back to that first season of coaching, the 1-12 record, the disappointment and stress of trying so hard to make the experience a memorable one for the kids, mine included. I had sworn off coaching, but had once again gotten the call that without a dad to step up, there might not be a team. So, I dusted off my clipboard and decided to give it another try. This time, I told myself, I'm going to relax. We were going to have fun, no matter what. I would focus on character. I would empower dugout leaders. I would let the team develop a culture that was fun and loose. We would laugh, and we would enjoy the beautiful game of baseball together.

I admit, I held some redemptive thoughts as well. If we were to be able to pull off this game, this victory, it could validate some of my choices and my egalitarian approach. I watched each pitch with tension, and each out meant the season's end was coming closer. At last, I watched the final pitch, the final out, and my eyes went up to the lopsided score on the board. This time, we held the larger number, and my players were cheering and hugging, and we were the Little League Fall Champions.

What Results Define Excellence in Coaching?

Is John an excellent coach now that he won the championship…or is excellence more than that? It certainly felt good to win and there's nothing wrong having that as a desire. That asks the question: how do we define excellence in coaching? How do we achieve the best results possible for our kids? Our survey results and live interviews with a wide range of coaches and parents indicated that winning was clearly secondary to skill development, both social and physical.

At ages 6-12, a strong emphasis on winning is not age appropriate. At that age, the emphasis should be on development of skills. Winning is not the key objective. Your goal is to help players love the game. Lots of times, kids this age are there to make friends, not win. Goals are a lot more than just winning. Love of game and developing skills are the most important things. You should ask the question: "why do you coach?" **If it's to win medals for your man cave, that's not a good reason to coach.**

–Don Showalter, USA Basketball

For many of our young players, excellence or top performance on the field or the court will include the dream of a kill shot to win the match, an extra-base hit with an amazing head-first slide into third base, or a three-point shot at the buzzer. Those dreams are natural–it's what kids see celebrated by high school, college, and professional athletes. They identify with heroes and role models. But those acts of stardom are the occasional rewards they may enjoy *after* they master the fundamentals. *Your role as a coach is to teach the fundamentals that underlie excellence.*

Do your kids want to shoot like Curry or distribute the ball like Rapinoe? Then the reality is that the fundamentals come first. It has been said that mastering any skill takes in general 10,000 hours of practice whether it be in sports, music, science, or the arts. Whatever the activity, impress on your team members how hard the stars or heroes that they observe have worked to perfect their skills. This is not meant to discourage them by any means. Actually, it is meant to establish a desire to become better and to develop a work ethic that will serve them well in other areas of their lives. Later in life, they can emulate the effort and the commitment that they have given to their sport.

The amount of time and energy available in the day or the week will vary by player. Young players have a lot on their plate and the amount of time you hope to get from them as a coach may be less than desired. The key is to meet each kid where they are at and to help them grow. That means paying attention to each player's physical strengths and weaknesses as well as working on group and team skills.

Not too far into the season and in early practice sessions consider having a short conversation with each of your players. What are the one or two skills that they are interested in developing? How do they view their strongest skills? What are those that they need to work on?

You have hopefully had enough time after two or three practices to observe each player and to have a sense of a goal or two they might work to address. You can spark the conversation with them if need be, with questions like: "How do you think we can develop your ability to guard another player or to play great defense? Let's identify the specific approach you can work on, for example footwork, balance, tracking the other player's body, not his or her eyes." Keep the description of what they need to do very basic.

For instance, we spoke with a father who coaches his five-year-old daughter's team in basketball. He shared a simple, yet profound discovery: the word "defense" can be too complex for that age group. It's not common kindergarten vernacular! Asking them to simply "stay in front of the player that they are guarding" may make much more sense to them at that age.

Imagery can help young players develop excellent habits, especially if the regular phrasing is a bit cumbersome. For example, fielding ground balls may appear simple but there's a lot to think about: glove down, knees bent, and eyes focused on the ball as it goes into the glove. Add to these the pressure of the moment, and it's easy to see why balls roll underneath their legs. One way to help reinforce effective techniques is to describe the activities like an alligator: fielding the ball with the glove, hand down and open, and the other hand comes down like the top of the alligator's mouth chomping down on the ball.

Breaking a player's skill development into these discrete chunks during the season will help him or her boost their physical performance and gain confidence through feelings of steady improvement. As appropriate, enroll their parents or siblings in mastering the skills in between organized practices.

Your role as a provider of positive feedback and encouragement to all involved is key to the foundation for the growth each child deserves.

Preparation and Practice Plans

Coaching excellence also means showing up prepared. Appearing to be disorganized to players and parents can go a long way to erode rather than build confidence. Come with a practice plan each time you work together. Include the other coaches in forming your plans or turn over segments of practice to your co-coaches.

Provide your players with an overview of what you'll be working on in a particular practice session and why. Give them a general road map up front so that they know what to expect. (You might mention that, after completing the basic drills, they will get to scrimmage at the end of practice!) This helps them know what to expect and builds players' confidence in you as their coach because they see that you know what you are doing.

A good friend and colleague of one of the authors offers the following example of how he sets *expectations for excellence* in all regards during the hockey season.

IYHA Bantam Team-4
Rules & Player Contract

<u>Playing Time Philosophy</u>

- Developing player skills is more important than winning each game.

- Playing time will be fairly divided–BUT– it is not guaranteed to be equal.

- Goalies will share playing time nearly evenly, but may get more time if they chose to "skate out" on days they are not in goal.

<u>Positions</u>

- Coaches will change player position assignments as we learn of the strengths and weaknesses of our team.

- We will also make changes to accommodate skill development. You may not get to play your favorite position.

<u>Practices: Monday Evenings and Saturday Mornings</u>

- Practice is more important than games. Please skip a game instead of a practice if you need to be absent.

- Arrive **30 minutes** before practice. Be ready (gear and skates on) **5 minutes** before we take the ice.

- Practice attendance will be taken. It will influence who sits and who plays in critical situations (power play, shorthanded, etc.).

Games: Monday or Thursday Evenings and Saturday Mornings

- Arrive **30-40 minutes** prior to the game. Be ready (gear and skates on) **10 minutes** before we take the ice.

- Coaches need **10 minutes** of undivided attention to review player positions and game plans.

- 1st period positions will be finalized **10 minutes** prior to game time. **Late arrivals will sit out the first period.**

Player Behavioral Expectations:

- Give 100% or your best at all times (practices & games).

- Listen attentively & follow advice of the coaches in practices and games. DO NOT ARGUE.

- No fooling around at practices (No playing with the pucks except as part of a drill).

- Repeated heroic, one-man efforts at the expense of teamwork are not tolerated.

- No criticism of teammates (on the ice, on the bench, or in the locker room).

- No profanity (on the ice, on the bench, or in the locker room).

- Problems with a coaching decision or a recurring problem with teammates' play will be discussed with coaches privately at an appropriate time (not in the heat of a game).

- No taunting opposing players before, during, or after the game. Keep your mouth closed when provoked.

- Always shake hands or bump elbows at the end of a game–no matter what has occurred.

- Retaliation, unnecessary roughness, unsportsmanlike conduct, or misconduct penalties will not be tolerated.

- Hitting from behind will *always* result in benching (even if the referee doesn't see it).

- Throwing sticks, gloves, helmets, water bottles or other items in disappointment will not be tolerated.

- Do not argue with, yell at, or make gestures toward the officials regardless of their decisions.

Escalating Consequences for Violating the Behavioral Expectations

Players who do not adhere to the behavioral expectations will be reprimanded. Consequences will escalate with each reprimand.

- Verbal warning: Laps/Ladders.

- Bench time: miss shift/miss game.

- Locker room behavior: Verbal warning; laps/ladders. Parent must be in the locker room at all times.

Equipment Needs

- Neck guards on.

- Mouth guard in the mouth.

- Sharpen skates approximately every 3 weeks.

I understand the Bantam Team 4 rules and understand the consequences for not following them.

Signature _____

Date _____

Your "Go To" Drills that Build Excellence

Whatever the sport you are coaching, the *go to* drills that teach the fundamentals are key to your effectiveness and style. Network with your co-coaches to develop your personal list of those fundamentals that you are most comfortable with. Divide and conquer when it comes to coaches taking charge of certain segments of practice. As a head coach, recognize the strengths of your peers and use them to the kids' and the team's best advantage. Feel free to place some level of responsibility on them to generate drills and activities that spark your team's development without abdicating your head coaching position. For instance:

> "Players, Coach Sam is our defensive specialty coach. He is most comfortable with teaching those skills and he will often be leading our drills when it comes to defense. Let's talk a bit right now about what defense is, what skills are part of being a strong defensive player, and how we can teach them to you."

Or,

> "Coach Cindy knows from experience as a volleyball player and a coach how to communicate effectively with each other during the match. We will be developing our own guidelines for how we call for balls, how we let each other know a ball is

being set for them, and who is rotating in or out between points. Our ability to communicate and use a common language is really important! It's as important in many ways as our physical game."

We heard in our interviews that great coaches help players love the game. This is why you coach–because you love the game and want to impart that to kids. Also, you coach because you see the big picture. We coach to build up young kids or young adults and show them lessons to be learned...challenging adversity and being a great teammate.

A cautionary note: introducing a skill that's too advanced can lead to frustration. For instance, trying to teach a 6-year old a 12-foot shot or a 30-yard pass – these are skills that they are simply not ready for. When things don't work, they may not want to participate in the sport anymore because they're not being successful. Allow each player to have success, and realize that their levels of tolerance for failure differ significantly. One player may continue to try a difficult move over and over while another may have only a couple of tries in them. Remember also that there are things that you can do to teach them a skill in stages. For basketball, this may mean dribbling in one place or while walking slowly...in baseball, tossing a tennis ball back and forth across a short distance...in soccer, playing with a lighter, smaller ball. Things often won't work well if you hit their frustration level.

Most of the kids love to play games in practice versus working on skills and drills. They can't wait for the time when they can scrimmage versus *just* working on drills and listening to the coaches bark out suggestions! With that in mind, build some portions of your skill development goals around competition that can include scrimmages. Be intentional about the skills you want them to practice. You might exaggerate the number of times players need to pass the ball before shooting or have everyone run the bases between scrimmage innings or set the ball a ridiculously high number of times before arriving at the "perfect set."

Finally, to develop trust as a coach, make sure you do what you say – that is, follow through. If you tell a player that he or she is probably going to play 10 minutes, then make sure he or she plays 10 minutes. If you tell players that the hardest worker in practice will get a prize, then make sure you follow through. If you never give the prize to him or her, they will have lost trust in you. Trust and humility needs to be demonstrated to the players.

Building Excellence Through Peer Feedback

An exercise that many youth coaches find effective at the end of a practice is to occasionally ask each of the kids what another player did well. You can do this in pairs with kids matching up across from each other in two lines or in a circle. The practice provides a great opportunity for the kids to reflect on how they performed in practice and why they appreciate each other.

The coaches can choose to model this process in an early practice if they wish, that is by providing a word or two for each player in front of the group that compliments their effort or performance in practice. "What I liked about what Cara did today was..."

A variation of this can be to have the coaches or the kids write a word or two about what they think the other players' strengths are. You can use 5 x 8 cards or sheets of paper with each kid's names. This can also be a mid-season or end-of-season appreciation exercise. For example, "What I appreciate about Joseph is his determination when holding onto his blocks in the line–he never gives up on the play".

As a coach, find something positive to say about each player. The influence you have as an adult over even some of the most recalcitrant of players may be much stronger than you think.

The Capstone

The end of season feedback to each player can also come in the form of a short note or letter to him or her from the coaches. For some of you, this may be a bridge too far, but for others it may be a welcome way to show appreciation to your players (and parents) and encourage them to continue to develop their skills. An experienced youth coach provides the following example:

Ken,

Just a note to let you know how much I enjoyed coaching you this year. I thought you were a great teammate and consistently encouraged other players especially when they made a mistake or felt down. Your last second shot to win the game against our rival will never be forgotten, and you should continue to cherish that moment!

In terms of fundamental basketball skills, I thought you improved tremendously rebounding the ball on the defensive end of the floor. Coming into the season, I'm not sure if you knew what a block out was and toward the end you were putting a body on someone on every shot attempt. Great job of learning! Because you improved that skill alone you were able to lead our team in rebounding. This was a great example of how hard work and a focus on the basics led to positive results.

Remember the most important lesson you learned this year and that was not to put your head down after a mistake. When you do that, the mistakes begin to compound. When a play is over, it is over…. onto the next one. This lesson will be an important one both athletically and in other aspects of your life. Good luck and call me anytime.

–Coach

Questions to Consider:

- How can you best provide developmental, end-of-season input to your players?

- What skills are you looking for in assistant coaches? How can you assemble the right team who can teach the young players all aspects of the game?

- What temperaments are you seeking in your assistant coaches?

- What are your coaching strengths and development needs? How can you set personal goals and improve? Who can serve as a mentor to you and your other coaches?

- How can you introduce the players and parents to the discipline and excellence you expect during both practices and games?

- What steps can you take to invite parents, siblings, teammates to practice skill development with your players in between practices? How can you reward this?

- And, most importantly, who is responsible for "excellence in drink boxes and snacks?" ☺

CHAPTER 7

How to Connect with Parents

*Role modeling is the most basic responsibility
of parents. Parents are handing life's
scripts to their children, scripts that in
all likelihood will be acted out for the rest
of the children's lives.* –Stephen Covey

The athletic director for a middle school relayed a sports story to one of our authors. She runs a leadership program for the student athletes in the school where she tries to help them apply their experiences with sports to real-world leadership and character topics. The students who take this program tend to be the leaders on their teams. At one session, she surveyed the group with a scenario: "Imagine a basketball game with time winding down on the clock," she said. "One shot will win the game at the buzzer. How many of you would want to take that shot?"

In this room of athletes, leaders, team captains,

and high achievers, only a few raised their hands. The athletic director was shocked by this. She assumed almost all would say that they wanted the chance to be the hero, to control the outcome, to be in that key position.

Afterwards, she asked a few of the students to explain why they did not raise their hands. What she learned and concluded was this: they were afraid of what the car ride home would be like if they missed.

While this is only one story, it speaks to a trend in our culture that some sports parents are putting enormous pressure on their kids to perform.

The Parent Challenge

Being a Catalytic Coach should mean that your relationship with the athletes' parents is a partnership based on shared expectations and support for each other. And yet, we've all seen when it can go horribly wrong. Viral videos and news stories of parents behaving badly make the rounds quite frequently. And we don't need to look very far to find our own examples of parents that become hyper-competitive, potentially unhinged, and who do damage to the efforts of a coach who is trying to build a positive culture. Is it happening at your ballparks, your soccer fields, your gymnasiums, or your volleyball courts? If so, it's enough to unnerve a new and inexperienced coach to the point where it impacts his or her psyche and could be a major reason so many parents choose to avoid coaching altogether.

Parent pressure and aggression is also taking its toll on umpires, referees, and other officials. Many sports leagues nationwide are concerned about a decline in the number of officials they can secure, and it seems harassment from parents (and to be fair, coaches) is a major factor.

> The National Association of Sports Officials conducted a national survey of more than 17,000 referees in 2017 and found that more than 70% of new officials quit within three years because of verbal abuse.

The severity of the problem is resulting in solutions that can be seen as extreme. *The New York Times* published an article a decade ago about the growing trend of "Silent Saturdays." According to the article: Silent Saturday is the name given to the day when parents are asked not to cheer or to guide their children in any way. There is no shouting, no yelling, no threatening the officials, or swearing at fathers from the opposing team. With the sidelines silenced, there is no pressure. The children are free to have fun. Sports leagues across the country have implemented this as a way to take a breather from the overwhelming noise pollution of parents *coaching* from the sidelines.

During the 2014 season, I asked my then 11-year-old son: "What do all the children in the dugout think when their parents urge them on with 'instructions' and 'encouragement' as they are playing the game?" He said bluntly, "they don't like it."

I further pressed him, "What about when I call out some last second reminders just before you bat, you know, the things we've talked about during the week and to help you remember what to do?" Again, he didn't mince his words and said, "Dad, it doesn't help."

He then went on to say, "When I am in the batter's box, I follow the instructions of my third base coach and put myself in the zone to block every other noise out. It doesn't help me, or any other kid when our parents are yelling things out."

I was staggered by his confident appraisal of the situation.

I went away and talked to a couple of players from our club who had played for Australia and in the MLB minor leagues. They said their fathers always watched them quietly and never said a thing. Let me say that again: never said a thing. They may have cheered when their son and his teammates made a nice hit or play, but they never put their own egos out there to think

It's our belief that very few parents want to be this way or be seen acting this way. For sure, there are some who are striving to live their own athletic dreams through their children, and who have little ability to control their worst competitive impulses. The good news for most of you reading this who are in recreational leagues, is that most of those parents tend to self-select into the ultra-competitive travel leagues and spend significant dollars traveling hundreds of miles to achieve recognition. The parents you likely work with at the recreational level don't want to be the parent who is viewed as a jerk. So, let's explore why this might happen, and what can be done to manage potential conflicts.

It Comes Down to Playing Time

Bottom line is this: parents want their children to succeed and possibly experience the thrill of making a game-changing play. That's been true since the dawn of time.

Simply put, we all want our kids to be successful in every endeavor, and in sports that means being a strong player and making contributions that both the parent and the young player can take pride in. We can all talk to ourselves about the power of character development and how losing can teach so many valuable lessons, and how it's really about teamwork, etc. But most parents want to see their kids smack a homer, make a basket, spike a winning point, nail the landing, and so on. It's a completely natural desire. At its root, we want our kids to have that chance.

This comes down to the all-important issue of playing time. One of our authors was almost paralyzed by the fear that parents would think their son wasn't getting enough playing time, the chance to pitch, the right number of at-bats, etc. Perhaps that's because as a parent, he wants the same thing for his child.

How does a coach manage the goal of giving every young player, no matter what his or her ability, ample playing time with the contrasting desire for the team to win?

Playing time is something a coach can directly address in pre-season communications. Consider how you will achieve balance, communicate that to both players and parents, and then stick with it. Most parents understand that in the most competitive games (i.e. playoffs, tournaments), the best players will probably see a bump up in playing time. Coaches have many different strategies for playing time – even keeping charts and graphs to ensure there is balance. In the *regular* season, coaches may be extra careful with playing time knowing that in the playoffs, it might be a bit more imbalanced. Overall, use an approach that you could explain when talking to any parents about their child's development.

"Why Are You Benching My Kid?"

Parents also have a fear that coaches might give up on their child. They are afraid that any mistake, any missed grounder, double-dribble, or false start could give the coach an easy reason to restrict playing time. In addition, what about when kids–yes, they are kids–misbehave, lose their focus, or let stubbornness get the best of them? Will this also give the coach justification to sit them on the bench and create a lasting impression that this young player is hard to coach?

So, you should be clear with your approach to discipline. Be careful to be consistent with every child (including yours) because fairness is something every parent pays attention to. Obviously, the approach for 6 to 7-year-olds would be different than dealing with 11 to 12-year-olds. As they get a bit older, *fairness* becomes very important to them. Being clear about how you plan to be fair will be critical to your players.

A key to developing relationships with both players and their parents is to focus on communication. Here are some important topics to cover initially with parents:

- As mentioned above, how will you ensure that playing time is fair and balanced?

- What are your strategies for discipline? Will you bench players, have them run laps after practice…and for what reasons can they be disciplined? (Again, this could impact playing time.)

- How should parents talk to you if they have an issue or disagreement? One strategy we learned in our interviews was a "24-hour rule:" parents should not discuss the game or a practice issue with the coach until 24 hours after it's over, especially if emotions are involved. This helps everyone have room to breathe and reflect.

- How can parents help you coach their kids, and their kids' friends? Giving parents roles helps everyone feel more connected to the team. Roles could include:

1. Snack/refreshments.

2. Social media.

3. Playing field preparation.

4. End of season activity.

5. Assistance with specific drills at practice.

6. Serving as an assistant coach.

Many coaches will work hard to develop initial messages such as these, but afterwards only send reminders of the schedule for games and practices. Consider going beyond this minimal communication. In-season messages can help remind parents of expectations that you have as a coach and can also provide you with a chance to make observations about the team's development. In short, you probably cannot over-communicate with parents!

How to Handle Disagreements

So, how do you handle the conversation with a parent, especially if it could get heated? Let's turn to the experts, namely a group of people who deal with frustrated parents all the time: school counselors.

According to confidentcounselor.org, here are some steps to keep in mind when having difficult conversations:

1. **Model appropriate behavior.**
   Use a calm tone and do not allow your voice to raise if they raise their voice. Continue to smile and speak calmly. Use non-threatening body language that shows that you are open to what they have to say.

2. **Validate their concerns.**
   Let them know right away that you understand that they are upset and you would like to help. Ask for more

information and let them know that you genuinely want to find a solution.

3. **Let them vent.**
Listen and nod while they vent. Sometimes they just need someone to listen. Letting them vent without being judged may be therapeutic for them.

4. **Don't take it personally.**
Remember that there are many reasons or motivations behind a parent's anger that often have nothing to do with you. Knowing this allows you to take a step back and moderate your emotional reaction.

5. **Use positive body language.**
Show you are interested in what they are saying. Eye contact and leaning in communicate openness. Be careful not to cross your arms or put your hands on your hips as these are seen as negative.

6. **Set limits and boundaries.**
You make the rules for the conversation. If an angry parent is shouting, you can tell them that you will not continue to listen unless they lower their voice. If they do not accept the boundaries, end the conversation and say that you will reschedule a time to talk when they are calm.

7. **Follow up with a personal phone call.**

Text and emails can be viewed as impersonal. Tone and emotion are often misunderstood in writing, so a personal call can be the best way to communicate with an angry parent. Calling may be a bit more time consuming in the short-term, but this is one of the most effective ways to improve coach/parent communication. Also remember, that in conversations that may be controversial, you may want to have another coach present with you.

While working with parents can give you a knot in your stomach, keep this in mind: put yourself in their shoes, and invite them to walk in yours as well. In almost every case, cooler heads will prevail. Practice empathy.

Regardless of how calm and cool you present yourself, sometimes you can't break through to parents. One of our interviewees explained that he was coaching football and a parent's son didn't understand the game. When he went to tackle, he closed his eyes. His dad wanted him to be a star football player, but the coach couldn't take the risk that he might put the young man in a position where he could hurt himself. The dad took his son to another team. In retrospect, that was probably the best decision for everyone concerned.

Most of the coaches we interviewed had success with parent relationships by having a meeting at the start of the year to lay out expectations and to clearly express goals for the players–fielding the inevitable questions that fathers and mothers have about the season.

Finally, the coach needs to determine what success means for his team and their competitive level in the sport. This should be discussed with the coaches as a group, defined prior to the season and reviewed as often as needed. Therefore, when parents have questions or concerns, as they certainly will, the coaching team can be on the same page.

We all know that parenting can be a daunting task. As coaches, appreciating the challenges that parents face and the anxieties that they have relative to their kids' experiences in youth sports, can help you and the parent work together to ensure they have a successful and gratifying team experience. Be kind. Be understanding. Be supportive.

Overtime: Closing Thoughts and Survey Data

Key Reasons You May Want to Coach Youth Sports

There are a lot of great rewards for being involved in coaching. If any of these resonate with you, then you may want to consider making the commitment to serve as a head or assistant coach in your community.

1. **You want to be part of your child's youth sports experience.** If you're a mom or dad who wants to coach and you can adhere to these reasons, then go be part of your child's world!

2. **You want to be a positive role model, something young players so desperately need.** Many coaches don't fully realize the impact they can have on young players' lives. It can be significant and lifelong.

3. **You love the game and want to pass that

love on to the kids. Spread the joy of playing a sport you love!

4. **You've seen coaches who are not very effective and you want to do your part to be a positive influence.** It's frustrating to stand or sit on the sidelines and see coaches who are clueless about motivating, challenging, and encouraging kids. Maybe it's time for you to step up and help?!

5. **You want to show kids that hard work and fun can go hand-in-hand.** They are not mutually exclusive.

6. **Although the coaching role is not solely to please the parents, you do care about helping them understand how they can be a positive voice in their child's sports experience.** Youth sports are just as much a learning experience for parents as they are for kids. Your example and positive voice can help the parents as much as their kids.

7. **You love competition and winning, but not more than you love to see young players develop.** Every coach wants to win, but youth sports coaches need to have as their number one priority the development of young athletes, both in character and in skill.

8. **You want to be part of your child's youth sports experience.** If you're a mom or dad

who wants to coach and you can adhere to the above reasons, then go be part of your child's world!*

Excellence in Coaching in Canada: A Look at a More Standardized Approach

Youth sports in the United States at nearly all levels are guided by local organizations that sponsor leagues. In some instances, they are sponsored by national sports associations that play a coordinating role. There are few national standards that are adopted for most or all sports across the country for kids. This is not always the case in Canada. In order to become a certified coach (each team must have at least one certified coach) you must go through a basic training process. The basics of skill development, child protection policies, and mental health concepts are addressed. We would encourage you to explore your local recreational and school resources to determine if there are state, regional, or local training programs available. This program is run in partnership with the Coaches Association of Ontario.

Sports Survey Overview

The survey was sent to a wide range of national coaches to gain their perspectives on coaching younger kids, primarily in recreational leagues.

---

* Adapted from a blog by Janis Meredith at Jbmthinks. https://www.winningyouthcoaching.com/tag/jbmthinks/

The introductory note to participants was as follows:

> You are invited to participate in a national study on coaching for youth sports. As a youth sports coach, no matter your experience, your insights and beliefs will offer a valuable glimpse into this important role. The survey should take 15-20 minutes to complete.
>
> Results of this study will be summarized to reveal best practices, common themes in coaching beliefs, and the principles that drive coaching in youth sports. Your voice matters and we appreciate your time in completing this survey.
>
> You may choose to answer anonymously or provide your contact information so that we may reach out to you for further conversation. Questions may be directed to Ben Cecchini at bcecchini@bencecchini.com.
>
> We appreciate your commitment to coaching and your dedication to young athletes.

To date, we have received 191 completed responses. The demographics of the survey participants were quite broad and are summarized below.

- 74% male; 26% female.

- 70% were between the ages of 36 and 55.

- 65% had recreational coaching experience; 35% had some travel league coaching experience.

- Approximately 50% of respondents had some level of teaching experience (outside of coaching)

- Approximately 50% had coaching training, eg, 3-4 hours or more.

- Nearly all respondents coached baseball or softball, basketball, soccer or football.

The survey questions were focused on what the coaches viewed as being important in coaching youth. We included in the book a number of themes and examples from the survey.

Listed below are sample questions from the survey:

- Describe your philosophy of coaching youth.

- Rate your level of confidence in coaching youth.

- When you think about a youth coach you admire what skills and qualities come to mind?

- Please list three words you hope your players would use to describe you as a coach.

- If you were to give 2 to 3 pieces of advice to new parent-coaches, what would you say?

- What resources or training would be helpful to you or your peers in becoming an excellent coach?

In addition to the survey results gathered via SurveyMonkey, we also conducted several in-depth interviews with coaches and parents. Specific themes and practical suggestions from those interviews are also included in the book's main sections, especially examples of practice exercises, sample notes to parents, methods of teaching the soft skills to younger players, etc.

Special thanks to those coaches who generously shared their time and ideas.

Lightning Source UK Ltd.
Milton Keynes UK
UKHW020628110822
407169UK00010B/1058